BODY MYTHS
BUSTED!

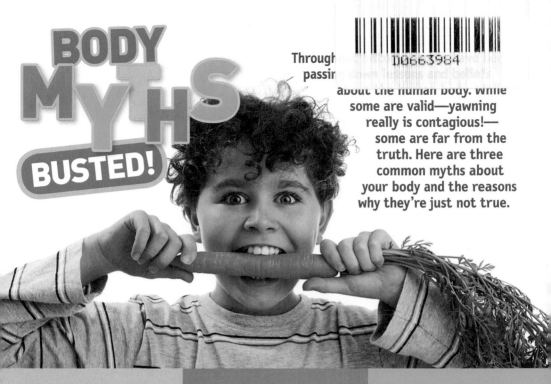

Through passir about the human body. While some are valid—yawning really is contagious!— some are far from the truth. Here are three common myths about your body and the reasons why they're just not true.

MYTH 1
Eating carrots improves your eyesight.

HOW IT STARTED
Legend has it that during World War II, British soldiers claimed to have excellent night vision because they consumed carrots. It was actually because of radar— the carrot bit was just used to confuse the Germans.

WHY IT'S NOT TRUE
Carrots do offer a high dose of vitamin A, which helps you maintain healthy eyesight. But eating extra of the orange veggies won't make you see better—only glasses can do that.

MYTH 2
Humans use only 10 percent of their brain.

HOW IT STARTED
In 1907, psychologist William James suggested that we only use a small part of our "mental and physical resources," which may have led to the 10 percent figure.

WHY IT'S NOT TRUE
Whether you're aware of it or not, your brain is firing on four cylinders almost all of the time—otherwise, you would stop breathing. Your brain activity slows when you're in a deep sleep or under anesthesia.

MYTH 3
If your ears are burning, someone is talking about you.

HOW IT STARTED
Ancient Romans believed that certain physical signs— including ringing or burning ears—were signs that some- one outside of earshot was chatting about you.

WHY IT'S NOT TRUE
Outside of having a sixth sense or bionic hearing, it's impossible to know when your name is coming up in someone else's conversation when you can't actually hear or see them talking. Besides, burning ears are usually a sign of sickness, sunburn, or overheating.

YOUR AMAZING

BODY!

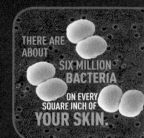
THERE ARE ABOUT **SIX MILLION BACTERIA** ON EVERY SQUARE INCH OF **YOUR SKIN.**

The human body is a complicated mass of systems—nine systems, to be exact. Each system has a unique and critical purpose in the body, and we wouldn't be able to survive without all of them.

The NERVOUS system controls the body.

The MUSCULAR system makes movement possible.

The SKELETAL system supports the body.

The CIRCULATORY system moves blood throughout the body.

The RESPIRATORY system provides the body with oxygen.

The DIGESTIVE system breaks down food into nutrients and gets rid of waste.

The IMMUNE system protects the body against disease and infection.

The ENDOCRINE system regulates the body's functions.

The REPRODUCTIVE system enables people to produce offspring.

Weird but true

MEN GET THE HICCUPS MORE OFTEN THAN WOMEN DO.

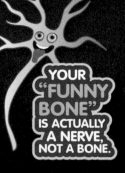
YOUR "FUNNY BONE" IS ACTUALLY A NERVE, NOT A BONE.

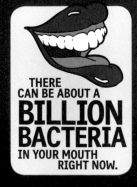
THERE CAN BE ABOUT A **BILLION BACTERIA** IN YOUR MOUTH RIGHT NOW.

All About YOU

66 PERCENT OF ONE OF THE CROWNS WORN BY THE QUEEN OF ENGLAND

26 iPOD NANOS

ABOUT 700 GUMMY BEARS

3,823 BLUE MORPHO BUTTERFLIES

.0000008956 PERCENT OF A CRUISE SHIP

A VERY YOUNG SIBERIAN TIGER CUB

AN INDIAN FLYING FOX

.000008309 PERCENT OF THE ST. LOUIS GATEWAY ARCH IN MISSOURI

A PAIR OF GLOVES WORN BY ASTRONAUTS ON A SPACE WALK

ONE TAI APOIN MONKEY

It would take
31,400 10-year-olds' brains
TO EQUAL THE WEIGHT OF A **sperm whale.**

* Based on an average 10-year-old kid's 3-pound (1.4 kg) brain. All other numbers also based on averages.

3

PLANETS

CERES

MARS

EARTH

VENUS

MERCURY

JUPITER

SUN

MERCURY
Average distance from the sun:
   35,980,000 miles (57,900,000 km)
Position from the sun in orbit: first
Equatorial diameter: 3,030 miles (4,878 km)
Length of day: 58 Earth days
Length of year: 88 Earth days
Surface temperatures:
   -300°F (-184°C) to 800°F (427°C)
Known moons: 0
Fun fact: Mercury travels around the sun faster than any other planet.

VENUS
Average distance from the sun:
   67,230,000 miles (108,200,000 km)
Position from the sun in orbit: second
Equatorial diameter: 7,520 miles (12,100 km)
Length of day: 243 Earth days
Length of year: 225 Earth days
Average surface temperature: 864°F (462°C)
Known moons: 0
Fun fact: Venus spins backward.

EARTH
Average distance from the sun:
   93,000,000 miles (149,600,000 km)
Position from the sun in orbit: third
Equatorial diameter: 7,900 miles (12,750 km)
Length of day: 24 hours
Length of year: 365 days
Surface temperatures:
   -126°F (-88°C) to 136°F (58°C)
Known moons: 1
Fun fact: Earth rotates 1.5 milliseconds slower every century.

MARS
Average distance from the sun:
   141,633,000 miles (227,936,000 km)
Position from the sun in orbit: fourth
Equatorial diameter: 4,221 miles (6,794 km)
Length of day: 25 Earth hours
Length of year: 1.88 Earth years
Surface temperatures:
   -270°F (-168°C) to 80°F (27°C)
Known moons: 2
Fun fact: A 100-pound (45-kg) person would weigh 38 pounds (17 kg) on Mars.

THERE IS NO GRAVITY AT THE CENTER OF THE EARTH.

This artwork shows the 13 planets and dwarf planets that astronomers now recognize in our solar system. The relative sizes and positions of the planets are shown but not the relative distances between them. Many of the planets closest to Earth can be seen without a telescope in the night sky.

SATURN

URANUS

NEPTUNE

PLUTO

HAUMEA

MAKEMAKE

ERIS

JUPITER

Average distance from the sun:
483,682,000 miles (778,412,000 km)
Position from the sun in orbit: sixth
Equatorial diameter:
88,840 miles (142,980 km)
Length of day: 9.9 Earth hours
Length of year: 11.9 Earth years
Average surface temperature: -235°F (-148°C)
Known moons: 66*
Fun fact: Jupiter weighs twice as much as all the other planets in the solar system combined.

SATURN

Average distance from the sun:
890,800,000 miles (1,433,500,000 km)
Position from the sun in orbit: seventh
Equatorial diameter: 74,900 miles (120,540 km)
Length of day: 10 Earth hours
Length of year: 29.46 Earth years
Average surface temperature: -218°F (-139°C)
Known moons: at least 62*
Fun fact: Saturn's rings are made of ice and rocks.

URANUS

Average distance from the sun:
1,784,000,000 miles (2,870,970,000 km)
Position from the sun in orbit: eighth
Equatorial diameter: 31,760 miles (51,120 km)
Length of day: 17.9 Earth hours
Length of year: 84 Earth years
Average surface temperature: -323°F (-197°C)
Known moons: 27
Fun fact: Some of Uranus's 27 moons are named for characters from William Shakespeare's plays.

NEPTUNE

Average distance from the sun:
2,795,000,000 miles (4,498,250,000 km)
Position from the sun in orbit: ninth
Equatorial diameter: 30,775 miles (49,528 km)
Length of day: 16 Earth hours
Length of year: 164.8 Earth years
Average surface temperature: -353°F (-214°C)
Known moons: 13
Fun fact: On Neptune the wind blows up to 1,243 miles an hour (2,000 kph).

*Includes provisional moons, which await confirmation and naming from the International Astronomical Union.

DWARF PLANETS

Haumea

Eris

Thanks to advanced technology, **astronomers have been spotting many never-before-seen celestial bodies with their telescopes. One new discovery? A population of icy objects orbiting the Sun beyond Pluto. The largest, like Pluto itself, are classified as dwarf planets. Smaller than the moon but still massive enough to pull themselves into a ball, dwarf planets nevertheless lack the gravitational "oomph" to clear their neighborhood of other sizable objects. So, while larger, more massive planets pretty much have their orbits to themselves, dwarf planets orbit the sun in swarms that include other dwarf planets as well as smaller chunks of rock or ice.**

So far, astronomers have identified five dwarf planets: Ceres (which circles the Sun in the asteroid belt between Mars and Jupiter), Pluto, Haumea, Makemake, and Eris. Astronomers are studying hundreds of newly found objects in the frigid outer solar system, trying to figure out just how big they are. As time and technology advance, the family of known dwarf planets will surely continue to grow.

CERES
Position from the sun in orbit: fifth
Length of day: 9.1 Earth hours
Length of year: 4.6 Earth years
Known moons: 0

PLUTO
Position from the sun in orbit: tenth
Length of day: 6.4 Earth days
Length of year: 248 Earth years
Known moons: 5*

HAUMEA
Position from the sun in orbit:
   eleventh
Length of day: 4 Earth hours
Length of year: 282 Earth years
Known moons: 2

MAKEMAKE
Position from the sun in orbit: twelfth
Length of day: 22.5 Earth hours
Length of year: 305 Earth years
Known moons: 0

ERIS
Position from the sun in orbit:
   thirteenth
Length of day: 25.9 Earth hours
Length of year: 561 Earth years
Known moons: 1

*Includes provisional moons.

SUPER SUN!

E ven from 93 million miles (150 million km) away, the sun's rays are powerful enough to provide the energy needed for life to flourish on Earth. This 4.6-billion-year-old star is the anchor of our universe and accounts for 99 percent of the matter in the solar system. What else makes the sun so special? For starters, it's larger than one million Earths and is the biggest object in our solar system. The sun also converts about four million tons (3,628,739 t) of matter to energy every second, helping to make life possible here on Earth. Now that's *sun*-sational!

THE SUN IS **400** TIMES LARGER THAN THE MOON.

The SUN'S surface is **9,932°F!** (5,500°C)

THERE IS **real gold** in the SUN.

Storms on the Sun!

Solar flares are ten million times more powerful than a volcanic eruption on Earth.

With the help of specialized equipment, scientists have observed solar flares—or bursts of magnetic energy that explode from the sun's surface as a result of storms on the sun. Solar storms occur on a cycle of about 11 years, with 2013 slated to be the most active year for these types of events. And while most solar storms will not impact the Earth, the fiercer the flare, the more we may potentially feel its effects, as it could disrupt power grids or interfere with GPS navigation systems. Solar storms can also trigger stronger-than-usual auroras, light shows that can be seen on Earth.

Some solar storms travel at speeds of **UP TO THREE MILLION MILES AN HOUR** (4.8 million kph).

Solar storm

COOL inventions

ROBOT DELIVERY

In 20 years, you might be able to walk back from the mall without carrying a bunch of bags, or go to the airport without lugging suitcases. The Cargonaut—just a concept for now—is a human-size robot that flies around picking up and delivering personal items. Containers called skyboxes would be available at Cargonaut locations in malls, airports, and hotels. To ship something ahead, you find a station, place your stuff inside a skybox, and punch in the Cargonaut location closest to your destination. That's where you pick up your package. The Cargonaut flies above the tops of buildings carrying your cargo. Meanwhile, your hands are free for more important tasks—like texting your friends about where you're off to next.

SPY PHONE

Even if you're not quite ready to join the CIA or Secret Service, you can still feel as stealthy as a spy. The MW2 is a watch that doubles as a cell phone. When you need to make a call—whether to phone in an important clue, or just to complain about your little brother's latest antics—simply dial the number on the MW2's keypad (or use the onscreen buttons), slyly lift your hand toward your mouth, and start talking. Your subjects will never know you're on the phone at all. They'll just think you're checking the time.

CLEVER
DOG WALKER

You just got home after a long day at school, and your restless four-legged friend is barking and running laps around your room. But it's cold and rainy, and the last thing you feel like doing is taking him for a walk. Relax. Lead your canine pal onto this JOG A DOG doggie treadmill, slowly turn the speed dial on the remote control to get things moving, and wait for him to work up to a trot. Fido gets a workout, and you stay dry.

SPACESHIP
FOR
TOURISTS

Prepare for liftoff! In the near future, you could be rocketing out of this world on Virgin Galactic's SpaceShip Two shuttle, the first to offer tourist trips to outer space. Leaving from a spaceport in New Mexico, an aircraft called the WhiteKnight Two will carry SpaceShip Two on its belly, taking off like a plane and climbing to 50,000 feet (15 km). At this height, the spaceship will drop off, turn upward, and zoom into space at a blazing 3,000 miles (4,828 km) an hour. Once you reach the starry blackness, you'll be able to see the curvature of the Earth below while you float weightless through the cabin. After hurtling in orbit for a while, the spaceship will turn and head back to Earth, touching down like a regular plane. It'll be a two-hour adventure of a lifetime.

SPACE Robots

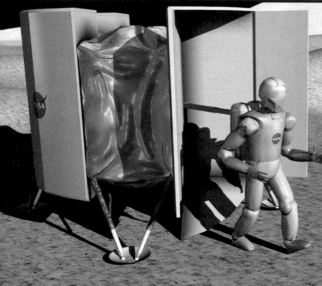

SOMEDAY YOU MIGHT CONTROL AN AVATAR ON THE MOON.

COLLECTING ROCK SAMPLES

Robot avatars may one day be handy companions to space travelers, whether they're as far away as Mars or as close as a space station or moon base. Though still a concept, robonauts, controlled remotely by humans, are expected to be a huge help to astronauts. "Our goal is for robots to work side by side with humans," says NASA's Matt Ondler. "Robonauts will help our astronauts with the three D's: jobs that are dirty, dull, and dangerous."

TO THE MOON

Someday, NASA hopes to send a humanoid robot, called R2, to the moon. Sending a robot to the moon will be far less expensive than sending a human. A robot is sturdier, can survive in tighter spaces, and doesn't need air. Even better, robots don't care how long it takes for NASA to return them to Earth.

Once on the moon, the robonaut could perform experiments, send live video back to Earth, and explore the lunar surface. R2 will be able to move using legs, or by attaching its torso to a four-wheeled rover and becoming part of the vehicle like a Transformer. And when R2's battery is low, it can plug into a solar-powered recharging station and get some much needed juice.

AVATARS IN SPACE

The future R2 would be designed to operate by itself. But for delicate and difficult tasks, a human operator would control it like an avatar in a video game. NASA will need people skilled at operating robonauts to ensure the success of future missions. So the next time your mom complains that you're spending too much time on video games, just tell her you're training for a job with NASA!

EXPLORING THE SURFACE

5 WAYS
You Use Satellites

Psst! Want in on a secret? Spaceships control our world! Well, not exactly. But much of the technology you use—TVs, telephones, email—relies on tons of satellites whizzing around Earth. Here's a look at five ways you use satellites.

1 TELEVISION If you've watched TV, then you've used a satellite. Broadcast stations send images from Earth up to satellites as radio waves. The satellite bounces those signals, which can only travel straight, back down to a satellite dish at a point on Earth closer to your house. Satellite transmission works sort of like a shot in a game of pool when you ricochet your ball off the side of the pool table at an angle that sinks it into the right pocket.

2 WEATHER News flash! A severe thunderstorm with dangerous lightning is approaching your town. How do weather forecasters know what's coming so they can warn the public? They use satellites equipped with cameras and infrared sensors to watch clouds. Computers use constantly changing satellite images to track the storm.

3 TELEPHONE As you talk back and forth with a relative overseas on a landline, you might experience a delay of a quarter second—the time it takes for your voices to be relayed by a satellite bounce.

4 EMAIL Satellites also bridge long distances over the Internet by transmitting emails. Communications satellites for phones and the Internet use a geostationary orbit. That means that a satellite's speed matches Earth's rotation exactly, keeping the satellite in the same spot above Earth.

5 GPS Driving you to a party at a friend's house, your dad turns down the wrong street. You're lost. No problem if the car has a global positioning system (GPS) receiver. GPS is a network of satellites. The receiver collects information from the satellites and plots its distance from at least three of them. Using this information, it can show where you are on a digital map. Thanks to satellites, you will make it to the party on time.

HOW A BASIC MOBILE CALL REACHES A FRIEND

You punch in a phone number and press SEND.

Your mobile (cell) phone sends a coded message—a radio signal—to a cellular tower, which transfers the radio signal to a landline wire. From there, the signal travels underground.

The underground signal reaches a switching center; there a computer figures out where the call needs to go next.

Through landlines the message reaches the cell tower nearest the call's destination.

Switched back to a radio signal, the call reaches the person you dialed. Let the talking begin!

WHAT IS THE "CELL" IN CELL PHONE?

A typical cellular, or mobile, tower serves a small area—about ten square miles (26 sq km). That area is called a cell. Whichever cell you are in when you make your call is the cell that picks up your data and sends it on.

Wildly Good Animal Reports

Velvety free-tailed bat

Your teacher wants *a written report on the velvety free-tailed bat. By Monday! Not to worry. Use the tools of good writing to organize your thoughts and research, and writing an animal report won't drive you batty.*

STEPS TO SUCCESS: *Your report will follow the format of a descriptive or expository essay and should consist of a main idea, followed by supporting details, and a conclusion. Use this basic structure for each paragraph as well as the whole report, and you'll be on the right track.*

1. Introduction
State your main idea.
> The velvety free-tailed bat is a common and important species of bat.

2. Body
Provide supporting points for your main idea.
> The velvety free-tailed bat eats insects and can have a large impact on insect populations. It ranges from Mexico to Florida and South America.
> Like other bats, its wings are built for fast, efficient flight.

Then expand on those points with further description, explanation, or discussion.
> The velvety free-tailed bat eats insects and can have a large impact on insect populations.
>> Its diet consists primarily of mosquitoes and other airborne insects.
> It ranges from Mexico to Florida and South America.
>> It sometimes takes refuge in people's attics.
> Like other bats, its wings are built for fast, efficient flight.
>> It has trouble, however, taking off from low or flat surfaces and must drop from a place high enough to gain speed to start flying.

3. Conclusion
Wrap it up with a summary of your whole paper.
> Because of its large numbers, the velvety free-tailed bat holds an important position in the food chain.

KEY INFORMATION

Here are some things you should consider including in your report:

- What does your animal look like?
- To what other species is it related?
- How does it move?
- Where does it live?
- What does it eat?
- What are its predators?
- How long does it live?
- Is it endangered?
- Why do you find it interesting?

FACT FROM FICTION: *Your animal may have been featured in a movie or in myths and legends. Compare and contrast how the animal has been portrayed with how it behaves in reality. For example, penguins can't dance the way they do in Happy Feet.*

PROOFREAD AND REVISE: *As with any great essay, when you're finished, check for misspellings, grammatical mistakes, and punctuation errors. It often helps to have someone else proofread your work, too, as he or she may catch things you have missed. Also, look for ways to make your sentences and paragraphs even better. Add more descriptive language, choosing just the right verbs, adverbs, and adjectives to make your writing come alive.*

BE CREATIVE: *Use visual aids to make your report come to life. Include an animal photo file with interesting images found in magazines or printed from websites. Or draw your own! You can also build a miniature animal habitat diorama. Use creativity to help communicate your passion for the subject.*

THE FINAL RESULT: *Put it all together in one final, polished draft. Make it neat and clean, and remember to cite your references.*

How to Observe ANIMALS

BOOKS, ARTICLES, and other second-hand sources are great for learning about animals, but there's another way to find out even more. Direct observation means watching, listening to, and smelling an animal yourself. To truly understand animals you need to see them in action.

VISIT

YOU CAN FIND ANIMALS in their natural habitats almost anywhere, even your own backyard. Or take a drive to a nearby mountain area, river, forest, wetland, or other ecosystem. There are animals in every natural setting you can visit. To observe more exotic varieties, plan a trip to a national park, aquarium, zoo, wildlife park, or aviary.

OBSERVE

GET NEAR ENOUGH to an animal to watch and study it, but do not disturb it. Be patient, as it may take a while to spot something interesting. And be safe. Don't take any risks; wild animals can be dangerous. Take notes, and write down every detail. Use all of your senses. How does it look? How does it act? What more can you learn?

RESEARCH

COMPARE YOUR own observations with those found in textbooks, encyclopedias, nonfiction books, Internet sources, and nature documentaries. And check out exciting animal encounters in National Geographic's book series Face to Face with Animals.

TIP:
Binoculars are a good way to get up close and personal with wild animals while still keeping a safe distance.

Love to watch animals? Check out these amazing animal and pet videos. video.kids.nationalgeographic.com/

COOL CLICK

Shark-Tracking ROBOT

"WAVE GLIDER" ROBOT

A robot that surfs on the waves is being used by scientists to track the movements of great white sharks.

H ow do you locate great white sharks in the ocean? You track them with a surfing robot, of course! That's what scientists are doing off the coast of California, U.S.A., in an attempt to keep tabs on the elusive sea creatures. The solar-powered "Wave Glider" robot—which looks a lot like a giant yellow surfboard—floats around in the Pacific Ocean picking up signals from tagged sharks up to 1,000 feet (330 m) away.

The signals are then sent by satellite to researchers on land who analyze the data to map out the sharks' whereabouts. That way they can get a better understanding of the sharks' daily lives and movements. Even cooler? All of the data picked up by the robot is available on a free app for iPods, iPads, and iPhones. Meaning you, too, can follow the ferocious fish with a swipe of your finger. Fierce!

Get Fit!

Try to work an hour of physical activity into each day. Whether you choose to play sports, go for a hike, or ride your bike, make your exercise exciting by switching things up and trying new ways to stay fit.

Exercise is awesome! Here's why:
- It makes you stronger and fitter.
- It makes you healthier.
- It makes you happier.

Ways to work out without even knowing it!

HOOF IT. Walk or bike short distances instead of riding in a car.

DO YARD WORK. Activities like gardening, mowing the lawn, and even shoveling snow are all great ways to burn calories—plus the fresh air is good for you!

STEP IT UP. Take the stairs instead of the elevators or escalators.

STICK TOGETHER. Get your friends and family together for a run, walk, or bike ride.

6 Tips for a Good Night's Sleep

Follow these tips for a solid night of zzz's—and a healthier you!

1. **Shoot for 10–11 hours** of sleep per night.

2. **Go to bed** around the same time every night. If you don't have a bedtime, set one for yourself and stick to it.

3. **Try to wake up** at the same time every morning. Even on the weekends.

4. **Keep your bedroom** quiet, dark, and cool.

5. **Turn off any extra lights** (or keep them in a spot where you can't see them). Charging phones and computer screens can be distracting as you try to fall asleep.

6. **Avoid caffeine,** like soda, tea, or chocolate, especially before bedtime.

BIZARRE Insects

Check out some of the strangest bugs on Earth!

The bright-colored head of the puss moth caterpillar warns predators to stay away. This species, one of the most toxic caterpillars in North America, can spray acid from its head when it is attacked.

puss moth caterpillar

walking leaf

The flat, green insect is a master of disguise: It's often hard to tell between this bug and an actual leaf, thanks to its large, feathery wings. This clever camouflage provides protection from potential predators.

giraffe-necked weevil

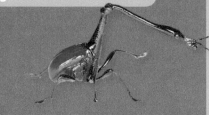

No surprise, this bug gets its name from its extra-long neck. The males have longer necks than females do, which they use to fight other males for mating rights.

thorn bugs

One tiny thorn bug may not be a match for a bigger predator, but when grouped together on a branch, these spiky bugs create a prickly pack no bird wants a bite of!

spiny katydid

This katydid is covered in sharper-than-kniv spikes. If a predator attacks, this species springs into action, defending itself by jabbing an enemy with its spiny legs and arms.

cockshafer beetle

The wild, feathery antennae on the male cockshafer may be cool to look at, but they're also helpful tools. They enable the bug to sniff for food and feel out its surrounding environment.

acorn weevil

The acorn weevil's hollow nose is longer than its body, and perfect for drilling through the shells of acorns. A female will feast on the nut by sucking up its rich, fatty liquid, and then lay her eggs in the acorn.

crab spider

Is it a spider or a crab? With its red-and-white coloring and pointy spines sticking out from its flat body, this arachnid looks a lot like a crustacean. But crab spiders stay on dry land, usually in the woods or in gardens.

man-faced stinkbug

There are more than 4,500 species of stinkbugs worldwide, including this brilliant yellow species, whose shield-shaped body displays a unique pattern resembling a tribal mask. Like all stinkbugs, this species secretes a foul-smelling liquid from scent glands between its legs when it feels threatened.

rhinoceros beetle

Ounce for ounce, this insect, which gets its name from the horn-like structure on a male's head, is considered one of the world's strongest creatures. It is capable of carrying up to 850 times its own body weight.

Stratos EXTREME Free Fall

One Giant Leap! Imagine standing at the edge of space and taking one giant leap before plummeting 24 miles (39 km) down to Earth below. That's just what professional skydiver Felix Baumgartner did as part of the Red Bull Stratos Project, setting a world record for highest and fastest parachute jump and becoming the first person to break the sound barrier without vehicle power in the process. But this jump wasn't just a daredevil's stunt: Scientists working on the project hope that they'll be able to advance aerospace technology that will help future space missions. Everything from Baumgartner's superprotective space suit to his high-tech parachute can be adopted by astronauts and scientists as they continue to explore life above Earth in the future.

MARS ROVER
CURIOSITY

MARTIAN LANDSCAPE

ANCIENT STREAMBED

SHINY SOIL
FOUND ON MARS!

Talk about a bright moment for Mars: A recent soil sample collected by NASA's rover Curiosity revealed shiny pebbles in the red planet's dirt. Scientists think the bright rocks are probably native Martian mineral flecks, and hope the sample will help them discover more information about the planet's terrain. So far, Curiosity, a six-wheeled robot about the size of a Mini Cooper car, has also stumbled upon an ancient streambed, indicating that water once flowed on Mars. These types of clues are helping researchers piece together whether the red planet ever supported life.

World Energy & Minerals

Almost everything people do—from cooking to powering the International Space Station—requires energy. But energy comes in different forms. Traditional energy sources, still used by many people in the developing world, include burning dried animal dung and wood. Industrialized countries and urban centers around the world rely on coal, oil, and natural gas—called fossil fuels because they formed from decayed plant and animal material accumulated from long ago. Fossil fuel deposits, either in the ground or under the ocean floor, are unevenly distributed on Earth, and only some countries can afford to buy them. Fossil fuels are also not renewable, meaning they will run out one day. And unless we find other ways to create energy, we'll be stuck. Without energy we won't be able to drive cars, use lights, or send emails to friends.

TAKING A TOLL

Environmentally speaking, burning fossil fuels isn't necessarily the best choice, either: Carbon dioxide from the burning of fossil fuels, as well as other emissions, are contributing to global warming. Concerned scientists are looking at new ways to harness renewable, alternative sources of energy, such as water, wind, and sun.

DIGGING FOR FOSSIL FUELS

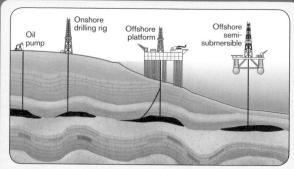

This illustration shows some of the different kinds of onshore and offshore drilling equipment. The type of drilling equipment depends on whether the oil or natural gas is in the ground or under the ocean.

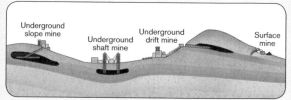

The mining of coal made the industrial revolution possible, and coal still provides a major energy source. Work that people once did using picks and shovels is now done with mechanized equipment. This diagram shows some kinds of coal mines currently in use.

LIGHTS OUT

In 2012, India experienced one of its worst blackouts ever, leaving some 600 million people in the dark. The blackout, which lasted a few hours, was caused by strain on an aging power grid. To avoid future blackouts, power needs to be delivered more efficiently. One possible solution? Focusing on alternative energy sources, like solar power and wind farms.

A train disabled by a massive power outage in India, July 2012

Alternative Power

WIND

Strong winds blowing through California's (U.S.A.) mountains spin windmill blades on an energy farm, powering giant turbines that generate electricity for the state.

HYDROELECTRIC

Hydroelectric plants, such as this one at Santiago del Estero in Argentina, use dams to harness running water to generate clean, renewable energy.

GEOTHERMAL

Geothermal power, from groundwater heated by molten rock, provides energy for this power plant in Iceland. Swimmers enjoy the warm waters of a lake created by the power plant.

SOLAR

Solar panels on Samso Island in Denmark capture and store energy from the sun, an environmentally friendly alternative to fossil fuels.

BIODIESEL

This Aero L-29 Delfin, nicknamed BioJet 1, was the first jet aircraft powered by 100 percent biodiesel fuel. Biodiesel—which can be made from vegetable oil, animal fats, or french-fry grease—is cleaner and emits fewer pollutants than fossil fuels do into the air.

Prehistoric
TIME LINE

HUMANS HAVE WALKED on Earth for some 200,000 years, a mere blip in Earth's 4.5-billion-year history. A lot has happened during that time. Earth formed, and oxygen levels rose in the millions of years of the Precambrian time. The productive Paleozoic era gave rise to hard-shelled organisms, vertebrates, amphibians, and reptiles.

Dinosaurs ruled the Earth in the mighty Mesozoic. And 64 million years after dinosaurs became extinct, modern humans emerged in the Cenozoic era. From the first tiny mollusks to the dinosaur giants of the Jurassic and beyond, Earth has seen a lot of transformation.

THE PRECAMBRIAN TIME

4.5 billion to 542 million years ago
- The Earth (and other planets) formed from gas and dust left over from a giant cloud that collapsed to form the sun. The giant cloud's collapse was triggered when nearby stars exploded.
- Low levels of oxygen made Earth a suffocating place.
- Early life-forms appeared.

THE PALEOZOIC ERA

542 million to 251 million years ago
- The first insects and other animals appeared on land.
- 450 million years ago (m.y.a.), the ancestors of sharks began to swim in the oceans.
- 430 m.y.a., plants began to take root on land.
- More than 360 m.y.a., amphibians emerged from the water.
- Slowly the major landmasses began to come together, creating Pangaea, a single supercontinent.
- By 300 m.y.a., reptiles had begun to dominate the land.

What Killed the Dinosaurs?

WAS IT AN ASTEROID OR A VOLCANO? These two common theories have been used by scientists to explain the disappearance of dinosaurs 65 million years ago. Researchers believe that a huge impact, such as from an asteroid or comet, or a massive bout of volcanic activity might have choked the sky with debris that starved Earth of the sun's energy. The resulting greenhouse gases may have caused the temperature to soar, causing half of the world's species—including the dinosaurs—to die in a mass extinction.

DINO TIMES

THE MESOZOIC ERA

251 million to 65 million years ago

The Mesozoic era, or the age of the reptiles, consisted of three consecutive time periods (shown below). This is when the first dinosaurs began to appear. They would reign supreme for more than 150 million years.

TRIASSIC PERIOD

251 million to 199 million years ago

- Appearance of the first mammals. They were rodent-size.
- The first dinosaur appeared.
- Ferns were the dominant plants on land.
- The giant supercontinent of Pangaea began breaking up toward the end of the Triassic.

JURASSIC PERIOD

199 million to 145 million years ago

- Giant dinosaurs dominated the land.
- Pangaea continued its breakup, and oceans formed in the spaces between the drifting landmasses, allowing sea life, including sharks and marine crocodiles, to thrive.
- Conifer trees spread across the land.

CRETACEOUS PERIOD

145 million to 65 million years ago

- The modern continents developed.
- The largest dinosaurs developed.
- Flowering plants spread across the landscape.
- Mammals flourished, and giant pterosaurs ruled the skies over the small birds.
- Temperatures grew more extreme. Dinosaurs lived in deserts, swamps, and forests from the Antarctic to the Arctic.

THE CENOZOIC ERA—TERTIARY PERIOD

65 million to 2.6 million years ago

- Following the dinosaur extinction, mammals rose as the dominant species.
- Birds continued to flourish.
- Volcanic activity was widespread.
- Temperatures began to cool, eventually ending in an ice age.
- The period ended with land bridges forming, which allowed plants and animals to spread to new areas.

ACE YOUR SCIENCE FAIR

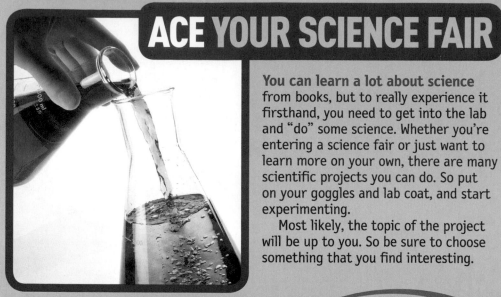

You can learn a lot about science from books, but to really experience it firsthand, you need to get into the lab and "do" some science. Whether you're entering a science fair or just want to learn more on your own, there are many scientific projects you can do. So put on your goggles and lab coat, and start experimenting.

Most likely, the topic of the project will be up to you. So be sure to choose something that you find interesting.

THE BASIS OF ALL SCIENTIFIC INVESTIGATION AND DISCOVERY IS THE SCIENTIFIC METHOD. CONDUCT THE EXPERIMENT USING THESE STEPS:

Observation/Research—Ask a question or identify a problem.

Hypothesis—Once you've asked a question, do some thinking and come up with some possible answers.

Experimentation—How can you determine if your hypothesis is correct? You test it. You perform an experiment. Make sure the experiment you design will produce an answer to your question.

Analysis—Gather your results, and use a consistent process to carefully measure the results.

Conclusion—Do the results support your hypothesis?

Report Your Findings—Communicate your results in the form of a paper that summarizes your entire experiment.

Bonus!

Take your project one step further. Your school may have an annual science fair, but there are also local, state, regional, and national science fair competitions. Compete with other students for awards, prizes, and scholarships!

EXPERIMENT DESIGN
Here are three types of experiments you can do.

MODEL KIT—a display, such as an "erupting volcano" model. Simple and to the point.

DEMONSTRATION—shows the scientific principles in action, such as a tornado in a wind tunnel.

INVESTIGATION—the home run of science projects, and just the type of project for science fairs. This kind demonstrates proper scientific experimentation and uses the scientific method to reveal answers to questions.

Printed in U.S.A.
14/KG/2